The Art of Dreaming

by

Matt Flumerfelt

Aakenbaaken & Kent

The Art of Dreaming

aakenbaakeneditor@gmail.com

ISBN: 978-1-938436-74-1

Stars

Stars caroling
through the crisp

music internal topic

softly to imbue
your hair with wishes

whose eyes are kissed
with tears.

Dream after and
likely

rain color create;

what mind is,
angels are more.

Blue Truth

Me telling eyes the
little about moon whom

from break of dawn
to dark of doom

ever rose upon a
tune of ivory

spilling blue truth;

benign and yet aloof,
impartial as the rain

that falls on every roof
without pity or disdain.

Clouds

Clouds speak softly
to the wind,
softly, softly whispering.
I think I hear them
call my name,
"Where have you been?"

Clouds speak softly
to the day,
soughing Syren-like
as if to say,
"Follow us and be free."

Aubade

The sun peeks through the early trees
or is it wee who peaks but never seas
clearly the traces cleverly concealed
of the love in every flower and field
and the bees that on industrious wing
cull the various colors of the spring
or the soft birds caroling their lays
simple sweet eternal vernal mysteries
as earth is broken by the iron plough
& apple blossoms dance upon the bough
for these signs of the revolving year
only to those who love plainly appear.

Inside-Out

Staring out from within,
yet caught
somewhere between the inside
and the out.

The further in you get,
the further out,
and it's hard to get ought
without getting caught.

Where does inside end,
outside begin,
if not in your own mind,
at your skin's fine line?

For Anaxagoras

The meaning of life is clear;
we're here for a reason.
And reason is the reason why we're here.

Listen good, 'cause I won't yell
or raise my voice a decibel:
the essence of existence is
to tell the truth and tell it well.
You can have reason on your side
and you will still be criticised.
Truth is universally applauded
and, in practise, wholly disregarded.
People tailor their perceptions
to fit their narrow preconceptions.
Many spend their lives assuming
because they think it's only human.

Our minds are designed for
occupations more worthwhile
than scrabbling for apples or
scraping coins together in a pile.

Ice Crystals

Tinder will kindle,
candles must burn.

Flowers will wither,
weather must turn.

Castles in winter
shiver in stone.

Icicles splinter,
chill to the bone.

Mockingbirds chatter,
sing out of tune.

What does it matter
now that you're gone?

Infinite Kiss

Am I the only
one who's lonely?
Maybe you
are lonely two.

Come with me
and you will see
that one and one
make three.

Then, when we
have made a trinity,
we'll hug and kiss
unto infinity.

Beauty's Fool

Lost in a maze
of winding ways
that never end,
I spend my days.

I have no clue
to lead me thro;
no spool of wool
to hold on to.

All I possess
to guide my steps
is a dream of
ideal loveliness.

Prayer

Lord have mercy
on my soul;
now it's broken,
make it whole.

Or if whole
you cannot make it,
then at least
please don't forsake it.

Save a blessing
for the day
when my soul
is cold and gray.

I Believe

I believe in dreams,
and I believe that dreams come true
if you really believe they do.

I believe in love,
and I believe that love is real
if love is what you feel.

I believe in clouds,
in their impassive majesty,
so effortlessly free.

Run with the Sun

If property
is not enough for me,
my stones,
and all my bones,

I'll have some fun,
be at one,
laugh at death,
run with the sun,

born in the morning,
dead in the evening;
live without mourning,
die without grieving.

Time Machine

I have something to say.
It won't take long.
I'll start without delay.
Listen, this is my song.

I had a dream.
What did it mean?
I took a ride
in a time machine.

The machine broke
and I awoke,
a bird sang
and the clock struck.

Ask Any Star

Ask any enlightened star
how many stars there are.

Ask any imaginative flower
whether beauty isn't power.

Ask a slowly drifting cloud
whether dreaming is allowed.

Ask a goldfish in a bowl
if it owns a golden soul.

Ask a hornet not to sting,
then come ask me anything.

Trial and Error

I shot an arrow
to win some marrow,
but the bones were hollow,
the end was sorrow.

In Re: Verse

If you plant a seed,
a tree will grow,
God or no.
If the soil is good,
pretty soon you'll have a wood
and lots of shade
where you can read
how the world was made.

Blank vs. Ink

Turn the page
and keep on turning;
a revelation
is the wage you're earning.

Out of nothing,
nothing comes;
no one nowhere
it's coming from.

Each blank page
is like the next
and every age
writes its own text.

Amor Fati

We are irrevocably
ourselves,
come time, or tide,
or death;
nor can a man unmake
what God perfects.

But willingly to be
ourselves,
sans health, or wealth,
and nothing else,
is truly wise
and happiness enough.

Let It Run

The world will still go on
when I am gone;
so let it run
and wake me when it's done.

The rose will still be red
though I am dead,
and poets sing
when winter turns to spring.

The world can go its way
and I'll go mine.
Perhaps one day
we'll meet. So long till then.

Here and Now

The guilty past
is dead and gone;
the trumpet blast
will never come.

A lover's smile,
a mother's woe;
heaven and hell
are here and now.

Give me strength
to carry on
until at length
my work is done.

Marsyas

Was there something in the satyr's flute
with heaven's music justly could compare;
could tempt a king his preference declare
against a god for one half man, half goat?

The king was not impartial, true.
Pan granted his golden wish
for helping Silenus out of a ditch;
but the Muses had their favorite too.

For hubris he was flayed alive,
for rank admits no rival,
but gives helpful hints on survival:
fawn on power or be crucified.

Blessed Be The Damned

Bury me in an unmarked grave
with Mozart, Paine, and d'Alembert.
What higher praise could I receive
than being damned with souls so rare?

Let other souls in comfort lie
if death has softer berths to give.
Grant them eternal rest, while I
remove whole rivers with a sieve.

While they with pious prayers make
obeisance to the Lord Almighty,
I'll have cake and tea with Blake
and feast on lines of timeless beauty.

It's All One

Heaven and hell
who can tell?
Where was man
before he fell?

If Adam
hadn't slept with madam,
kids—they would have
never had 'em.

Sorrow and joy,
pleasure and pain,
heaven and hell,
all are the same.

Love Power

The love of beauty
and the impotence of art
divide my heart
and strive for unity,

where love is power
and power is thought,
and truth unsought
opens like a flower,

and pleasure and pain,
laughter and tears,
my hopes and fears
blend like earth and rain.

A Crash Course In Enlightenment

Buddha stood up on the rostrum,
a man who overdosed on pork,
to give the lesser monks a sermon
and try to spark enlightenment.

Instead of lecturing on metaphysics,
he simply lifted up a flower,
which some there took to stand for truth,
but really, it was just a flower,
and that's the truth.

I guess truth is when things
only stand for themselves.
Otherwise, everything becomes a symbol
for something else and pretty soon
nothing means anything.

I wonder if the Buddha,
the Awakened One, had held up
a crushed beer can or a piece
of the Berlin wall, would it have had
the same effect?

The mind likes symbols
and it's all one anyway.
Maybe enlightenment is where
everything stands for everything,
where flowers are bullets
and victory means peace.

The Greeks had wise men too.
Legend tells about Sciron,
a bully who lived by the sea
and forced passing travelers
to wash his feet. When they
bent over to comply,
he kicked them over the cliff,
where they were devoured by a huge turtle,
teaching enlightenment
by hurling people to their deaths.
The Chinese method wasn't quite as strict.

One time, a seeker of the Way
came to a famous Zen master and asked,
"Venerable master, how can I become
a Buddha?" The master shrugged and
answered,
"You tell me."

Great Moments In History

The Nile river overflows its banks,
Samson breaks his chains,
prisoners escape from Alcatraz,
Vesuvius erupts and buries Pompeii,
Vandals sack the Roman capital,
Hitler's art school application is rejected,
Stanley locates Livingstone,
Laurel meets Hardy,
Abbot and Costello meet the Wolfman,
Beauty meets Mr. Vinyl,
Dante chooses the vernacular,
Petrarch finds a rare palimpsest,
Baudelaire catches syphilis,
Schubert catches syphilis,
Nietzsche catches syphilis,
Abelard gets castrated,
Bruno gets burned, Galileo recants,
Caesar sets fire to the Alexandrian library,
the Civil War gets uncivil,
Hitler writes *Mein Kampf* and lights a kampfire,
things fall apart, the center cannot hold,
Alexander Pope writes *The Dunciad*,
several dunces read it,

Conrad finds the heart of darkness,
Wordsworth recollects emotion in tranquility,
Robert Burns consumes John Barleycorn,
Kublai Khan decrees a pleasure dome,
Freud discovers cocaine and the Id,
Custer wishes he had stayed in bed,
Spinoza gets excommunicated and finds God,
Louis Pasteur improves the taste of beer,
Schliemann excavates Troy, nine times,
Elgar composes *Pomp and Circumstance*,
Zappa composes *Peaches en Regalia*,
Picasso gets his first box of Crayolas,
the Sibyl celebrates her thousandth birthday,
young master de Sade gets a whipping,
and likes it,
Max Planck discovers something or other,
Schopenhauer thinks the world is his idea.

History, my friends,
is the random accumulation
of facts, arbitrarily selected
for studious reflection,
pasteurized, homogenized,
sterilized and disinfected,
distilled, filtered,

ozonated and irradiated,
strained and sifted,
served up like a vintage wine
or French confection,
a work of scholarly perfection,
a miracle, a book without a spine.

My Nitty Gritty Kitty

I gave her a diamond ring,
but she hocked it;
gave her the key to my heart,
but she lost it.
She's my pretty little
nitty gritty kitty.
I need her like sinners need hell.

I wrote her a poem,
she laughed in my face.
She doesn't have time
to waste reading that trash.
She's my pretty little
nitty gritty kitty.
I need her like addicts need crack.

My kitty ran off
with some dude from the keys
who lives on a boat
and likes cocaine and jazz.
She's my pretty little
nitty gritty kitty.
Damn that bastard, whoever he is.

Poetic Prodigy

When I was just a kid,
banging against my crib,
sucking on my mammy's tit,
I knew I was a poet.

My gibberish was eloquent
compared to every other runt.
I learned my ABC's
as easy as you please.

Moved on to Dr. Seuss
and Mother Goose,
the Brothers Grimm
and *Huckleberry Finn*.

Before long I was
reading *War and Peace*,
a book six inches thick
at least.

Read Juvenal
while in my teens
and Freud and Jung
on sex and dreams.

Reading hour after hour,
I mastered Kant and Schopenhauer;
thought Augustine was disgusting,
but Nietzsche has a lot to teach ya.

Since I planned
to be an author,
I read Chaucer
and the *Morte d'Arthur*.

If you're wondering
what I'm getting at,
I'll keep it short,
I know it's late.

Life is a war
of all against all
in which the prize
is almost always trivial.

It's not my job
to change your behavior.
I'm just a poet,
not the world's savior.

But if I pickle you in verse
like a fetal pig in formaldehyde,
don't pitch a hissy fit or cuss
unless you damn your own dumb hide.

Love Poem

I'm Teddy Roosevelt and his
Rough Riders rolled into one.
I want to charge your San Juan Hill
and storm your Bastille.

I want to be the asp you clasp
to your naked breast,
whose venom makes you gasp for breath.

The universe began with a bang.
Evolution started with a jolt.
It took lightning to jump start Frankenstein.
Let me shock you with my thunderbolt.

Let my rough winds shake your darling buds.

Philosophers would shit can truth
if they could chew your juicy fruit.
Saints would ditch their Paradise
to win the bliss between your thighs.

Pleasure is the bait you dangle
from the fishing pole of love,

and I'm the fish for which you angle,
the Moby Dick you're dreaming of.

Karmic Calculus

There are strange sights
in paradise,
unparalleled in deepest hell
by ghastly devils packed in ice.

For although hell's
a downright wicked place,
this Eden is a dunghill of disgrace.

Adjust your gaze
and you will see earth's tenants
doing penance
in a multitude of ways.

Chasing madly after money,
we waste our lives,
like ants, or bees collecting honey
and guarding our hives.

Others, in vain
pursuit of pleasure,
reap the pain
of pampered leisure.

For every crass act we commit,
every frailty of nature,
there's a condign punishment,
a form of self-inflicted torture.

Immortal Desire

Be my Rosetta stone;
let me decipher your hieroglyphs.
I want to learn the secret
language of your heart.

Let me transcribe
your cryptic, Coptic,
demotic, demonic yearnings
for my priapic stirrings.

Let me be the obelisk
to your odalisque.
I'll be your pharaoh,
you can be my queen.

Pericles had Aspasia,
Alexander had Thais,
Antony had Cleopatra,
Abelard had Eloise.

We'll take a pleasure barge
along the Nile,
and when we get the urge,
we'll fuck awhile.

Then, when we die,
we'll lie in state
in a private pyramid,
and our souls will copulate.

Here We Go Again

The Antichrist is on his way,
so pious crones assert with furtive joy.
The paparazzi got the dope
straight from the Pope.
John Paul saw a bat again
flitting through the Vatican
and said, "Aw hell, not that again!"

Some psychic nun
has seen a vision,
a lucky omen:
this time Christ will be a woman!

Fueling all this speculation
is Ken Starr's investigation.
Thanks to Bill and Monica,
Wall Street could collapse by Hanukah,
triggering worldwide depression,
while those who play the game cash in.

This poverty and hunger
will allow some power-monger,
some ruthless demagogue
to set the foolish world agog.

While the rabble babble on
from Babylon to Avalon,
he'll organize his war machine,
the hero of the common man.

By enacting legislation
he'll complete our degradation,
crushing freedom by degrees.
Poets will be public enemies.

Crowds of Jesus lookalikes
sporting beards and Birkenstocks
will be spouting Bible verses
while old ladies clutch their purses.

The year 2000 is upon us.
All you kooks with names like *"Mabus"*
had better know your Nostradamus,
read Karl Marx and watch for comets.

If the devil spawn takes over,
all I ask is one small favor:
if I'm not around, politely
tell the Antichrist to bite me!

Tribute to Li

Sad night the poet Li Po drowned.
While trying to embrace the moon,
his tipsy *bateau ivre* overturned,
quenching the laughter of his pen.

To My Beloved

I will love you better than
any other lover ever can.
I'll keep your heart inside a jar
preserved in honey mixed with myrrh.
Our love will be embalmed forever
in memory, etched in time's ledger.
My love for you is hard as bone,
soft as spider silk or eiderdown,
white as winter, warm as dawn,
rich as rosewood, gentle as a fawn.
I'll bend my skill to dry your tears.
Word-bracelets bind my heart to yours.
And when my sight begins to fail,
I'll celebrate our love in Braille.

The Perfect Lover

Everywhere we go on our
excavations into truth,
we leave our toothmarks
on the fossils we unearth,
the thighbone of some mastodon,
proving that it's meat we crave,
not understanding.
These canine teeth we have
were not given us for nothing.
They were meant to pierce
the skulls of infants
and lend charm to our
expressions of remorse.

Whenever we exhume
some crumbling cadaver,
crispy as a french fry
from baking in the sand
for centuries or tough
as whang from curing
in some Andean cave,
it's our own face we find
behind the bandages.

The blind and giant eye
of science turns its blank stare
on our private despair,
but the mind behind the camera
sees our shame as fair game
and exploits our pain for gain.

A sunbeam trickles down
the world's surface
and impregnates some germ
lying leeward on a leaf.
The zygote responds.
The pupa shucks its husk
and proclaims a downy moth.
It bats its wings for practice,
then flutters like a rapid,
muffled drum to the beat
of its own palpitating pulse.

Yo bro! I ain't too proud
to do blow, but hey:
who needs the trouble?
I don't live in no bubble,
don't use no pick and shovel.
If you need a dollar,

don't pray to Allah or the
Dalai Lama. They won't
put no cash in yo wallet.
Don't do like Jeffrey Dahmer
or the Unabomber. Man,
those zeros ain't heroes.
Those hoods got the juice
that'll turn yo ass loose.
You'll wind up in jail,
some stinkin' hell-hole
in a room wif some dude's
got his pecker tattooed,
some burned-out ol' fool
wif his hand on his tool
sayin': "Come to me sugar,
come to your Dad." A
Casey Jones junkie
wif snakes in his head.

People, this is America.
We invented freedom.
We live for it and we're
willing to die for it.
I pity the poor sonofabitch
who ever tries to take it

from us. Why do you think
we drink too much, fight
too much, drive too fast,
carry guns, shave our heads,
wear tattoos, pierce our
tongues, and quit our jobs?
Because no one can stop us.
Who needs the Eiffel Tower?
We had Eisenhower. And we
never hesitate to tell our
leaders that they work for
us and not the other way
around. We complain a lot,
but we always get the job
done. Maybe we're not too
refined, but refinement
never paid the bills, won
a war, or made your lover
beg for more.

When all our explorations
come to an end, we discover
we've created ourselves in
our own image, the perfect lover.

Fatal Flaw

Winter, mad as a March Hare,
was finally making its departure.
The frenzied snows of yesteryear
had gone, no one knew where.

Winter's bite was bitter.
The Cold War raged post Hitler.
But after the near fatal flaw,
there came a thaw.

But the kingdom didn't come.
The peace dividend
met an untimely end,
a victim of hit and run.

Solomon's Seal

I'm the sun and moon,
the son of man,
the one man,
the only one,
the soul man.

The universe conspired
to create me.
I took eons of evolutionary
engineering to assemble.
Still unsure of what I am
or what I'm supposed to do,
I try to love my brother man,
but always give the devil his due.
I pity Jesus on the cross
but love the rattle of the dice.

When people attempt to become gods,
they always immolate themselves
and use their acolytes for firewood.

Oh, the herbivores will inherit
the earth alright, but not until
the carnivores have sucked it dry.

Truth can be brutal,
but the fact you ignore
will bash in your skull
and break down your door.

Vice hates virtue and vice versa.
For every Jesus there's a Judas,
every Caesar has a Brutus.

We pass the time
on our way from birth to death
trying to guess3
the meaning of success.

We're waitin'
for the big showdown with Satan,
a hoedown with Abaddon
on the plain of Armageddon,
followed by a thousand years of peace,
thanks to the ubiquitous police.

Success, for me, is easy to define:
I want to touch a nerve with every line.
I want my words to galvanize your mind
and raise the curtain on this pantomime.

Our puny race
is struggling to evolve.
We've learned to procreate
but not to love.

But don't give up,
there's still a ray f hope,
'cause I'm the sun and moon,
the son of man,
the one man,
the only one,
the soul man.

The Skies Over America

The skies over America
are vibrant as a Pollock painting
and dissonant as a Schoenberg
symphony. They're the canvas
on which we scrawl the graffiti
of our lives.

Ours is a garden where
every flower may flourish,
bitter nightshade and evening
primrose, a Mendelian greenhouse
where hybrids are the rule
and whore lies down with priest.

We're enamored of the camera.
If we could, we'd like to film
the destruction of the world,
even though no one would be left
to watch it explode a second time
except a few seagulls.

America was born to immigrant
parents in a sharecropper's shack.
Three acres and a mule were its
only possessions. It was suckled
on hard work, cheap whiskey,
tobacco, cornbread and collard greens,
and the promise of eternal life.

The skies over America
are crumbling. They're responding
well to therapy. They need
more antioxidants, plastic surgery,
yoga lessons. They're weeping.
The skies over America are
closed for remodeling.

Day of Wrath

Day of wrath,
that horrible day
will turn Earth to ash;
so David and the Sibyl say.

What a rumble will go down
when the Judge comes to town
to whom all things are known.

The trumpet,
diffusing an amazing tune
through every tomb on the planet,
will bring all flocking to the throne.

Death and nature
will be suspended
when all mankind resurfaces
to answer the Judge.

A book will be produced
in which everything needed
to judge the world is written.

When the Judge sits down, therefore,
whatever was hidden will appear.
He'll clear his calendar.

What will a peon like me say then?
What lawyer will take my case
when even the just are hardly safe?

King of tremendous majesty
who saves the elect for free,
wellspring of compassion, save me.

Remember, dear Jesus,
I'm the reason for your journey.
Don't forsake me on that sad day.

Seeking me, you sat down weary.
Suffering the cross, you redeemed me.
A laborer is worthy of his pay.

Judge who punishes fairly,
grant the gift of remission
before the day of reckoning.

I groan like someone in jail.
My face burns with shame.
Spare your suppliant, God.

He who absolved Mary
and gave the thief a hearing
has given me hope as well.

My prayers are unworthy,
but Thou who art good,
kindly arrange matters such
that I don't burn in eternal fire.

Prepare me a place among your sheep
and fence me off from the goats.
Reserve me a spot way over on the right.

When the cursèd are thwarted
and with searing flames rewarded,
call me with the blessèd.

I beseech you, kneeling in prayer,
my heart charred to a cinder,
watch lovingly over my final hour.

Tearful the day when guilty man
rises from the ashes
to be judged. Pardon him then,
O God. Merciful Lord Jesus
give them rest. Amen.

The Art of Dreaming

One day, the sun sowed its seeds
and a swan sang its song at dawn
among rushes. The song reads:
"Eve is dreaming of a better Adam,
night is dreaming of a brighter day."

Musing by the stream,
I had some time
to let my mind unwind
and unravel the riddle
of my life a little.

I realized that
more than anything,
I want the chance to sing
and turn my hand to verses;
boneheads to rhyming curses,
mermaids to sweet wet nurses.

I also came to see
beneath the trees that day
that a person is a poem
speaking itself into existence,

blending thought and feeling
till they mingle in a single stream of meaning,
for that's the art of dreaming.

A Routine Excavation

I found what might have been
a bust of black obsidian
resting in a desert basin
while on a routine excavation;
a misshapen stone with
curious carvings on it;
a runic text or funeral stele
where some pharaoh or literary fellah
engraved the lessons gleaned
from hard experience.
It seemed a venerable head,
a solid chunk of diorite or
some translucent mineral with rich veins
of pyrite running through;
a skull once filled with wisdom.
The same laws or rules of art
that compound crystal from fine sediment,
no doubt intrigued this shiny globe of darkness,
this urbane orb or glacial stowaway
fraught with ancient motives.

Flower

All my dreams are of sun
and leaves and love,
grass and trees, a breeze
and someone fun;

of peace and youth,
a beach and truth;
of falling asleep together
and never losing touch;

of growing old but
never growing up.
All my dreams are of
me and you, and us.

Distant Touch

Because there were stars
that let fall time and tears
and were soft as a rose
as the snow said its prayers,

and because they could speak
and knew you would hear,
though their voices were weak
and they lived rather far,

"Your touch was enough,"
they said, "to remind us
not equations but love
is the stuff we're made of."

Fragments

I can but choose,
and never do
what no one does;
that is, I never can create
what never was.

II

Plato was right,
poets *are* parasites,
but *The State*
killed Socrates, not poets.

III

Love is a subtle chemistry
whose elements are you & me,
joined in a novel synthesis
and consummated with a kiss.

IV

Now the splendid day the whole year through
is bent upon the bough with summer's hue,
attended by a myriad array
of hours and powers the seasons to renew,
as every care is spirited away.

V

You are my wealth
and you my only fame;
for two who love
have nothing more to gain.

VI

Once having been,
a man must always be.
To live but once
is immortality.

VII

Love is the reason
for this passion play.
Two souls collide,
struggle briefly and subside,
never knowing why,
and love is the reason.

VIII

Life drives us
into each other's arms
to find safety
from the world's alarms.

IX

When spring returns with sunny weather,
the weeping rose will soon recover;
timid birds will sing together
and tread the air with daedal feather.

X

The factory where the soul is built
is innocence and guilt;
where consciences are bought and sold,
some for love and some for gold.

XI

Look in your soul
and see what's written there;
open the scroll,
the truth is hidden there.

XII

Good is evil,
evil can be good,
and the devil
treats us as he should.

XIII

Imagination, that flower of the mind,
is blasted by unseasonable fears,
and in the ruin of relentless time,
it grows more slowly, watered by our tears.

XIV

Woe to the unwary
who look for mercy,
for they will find
mankind's not kind.

XV

Light is the golden life
of every living thing;
heavy the night of grief
that wakes us from our dream.

XVI

We travel to the stars
on a trelliswork of tears,
scale the skies
on a scaffolding of sighs.

XVII

We sin against
the tyranny of death
in bringing forth
a little loveliness.

Each fragile flower
striving in the light
needs second sight
to consummate its power.

XVIII

The universe isn't a place,
it's Nirvana, a state of nothingness,
where outer space and inner peace
are one, time and distance don't apply,
and truth is a spinning coin.

XIX

Thro pain we learn to love,
when pain is o'er;
for love is but the pain
we felt before.

The bliss of innocence
gladly we forgo;
take arms in our defense
to win us woe.

XX

While the weary world unwinds
to its foregone conclusion,
man rewrites stale line by line
the epic of his own decline,
believing every rhyme pristine.

XXI

The purpose of law,
as Nietzsche saw,
is to save the lamb
from the lion's claw.

XXII

How, when thought's remiss,
can I dismiss
as show and nought my bliss?
For thought alone has power to express.
And yet, when thoughts arise,
I never criticise;
for thought can make men wise,
and happiness within this power lies.

XXIII

We drank from the same glass
and ate from the same plate.
Like two blades of grass,
we shared the same small plot.

XXIV

Spring is a greeting,
winter a farewell.
Innocence is fleeting,
impossible to recall.

XXV

History, if anyone's left to write it,
will watch us push the boulder
like Sisyphus toward the summit,
knowing then what fools we are and were.

XXVI

Lock truth in a cage,
it praises ceilings, bars and floors,
but set it free to roam at large
and every verse unearths a universe.

XVII

You a die and me a die,
we shook our dice together,
but two deaths don't make a life
unless love throws them there.

XVIII

In the midst of love,
we're in the midst of war;
it starts out nice enough,
but often ends as a *bête noire*.

XXIX

It's true, the stones
have not much to do,
but if we knew
the effort they exert
to seem so inert,
we'd envy their art.

CPSIA information can be obtained
at www.ICGtesting.com
Printed in the USA
FSHW020902010620
70453FS